P9-DFI-459

what NOW?

Help for Pregnant Teens

Linda I. Shands

InterVarsity Press
Downers Grove, Illinois

InterVarsity Press® is the book-publishing division of InterVarsity Christian Fellowship®, a student movement active on campus at hundreds of universities, colleges and schools of nursing in the United States of America, and a member movement of the International Fellowship of Evangelical Students. For information about local and regional activities, write Public Relations Dept., InterVarsity Christian Fellowship, 6400 Schroeder Rd., P.O. Box 7895, Madison, WI 53707-7895.

All Scripture quotations, unless otherwise indicated, are taken from the HOLY BIBLE, NEW INTERNATIONAL VERSION®. NIV®. Copyright © 1973, 1978, 1984 by International Bible Society. Used by permission of Zondervan Publishing House. All rights reserved.

Cover photograph: Dale Durfee/Tony Stone Images

ISBN 0-8308-1967-3

Printed in the United States of America ∞

Library of Congress Cataloging-in-Publication Data

Shands, Linda, 1944-
    What now? : help for pregnant teens / Linda I. Shands.
        p. cm.
    Includes bibliographical references.
    Summary: A guide written from a pro-life perspective for unmarried pregnant teenagers.
        ISBN 0-8308-1967-3 (alk. paper)
        1. Teenage mothers—United States—Juvenile literature.
    2. Teenage pregnancy—United States—Juvenile literature.
    3. Pregnancy—Religious aspects—Christianity—Juvenile literature.
    4. Pregnancy, Unwanted—Decision making—Juvenile literature.
    [1. Teenage mothers. 2. Pregnancy. 3. Unmarried mothers. 4. Christian life.]
I. Title.
HQ759.4.S5   1997
306.874'3—dc21   97-26149
                                                                           CIP
                                                                            AC

| 18 | 17 | 16 | 15 | 14 | 13 | 12 | 11 | 10 | 9 | 8 | 7 | 6 | 5 | 4 | 3 | 2 | 1 |
| 11 | 10 | 09 | 08 | 07 | 06 | 05 | 04 | 03 | 02 | 01 | 00 | 99 | 98 | 97 | | | |

A Letter from the Author *9*

1 What Am I Going to Do? *13*

2 What Is It Like to Have a Baby? *21*

3 What Will Having a Baby Cost? *33*

4 What About My Baby's Father? *39*

5 Should I Live with My Parents? *47*

6 Can I Make It on My Own? *55*

7 Should I Choose Adoption for My

Child? *64*

8 What If I Choose to Raise My Child? *74*

9 How Can I Live with My Choice? *83*

Just for Parents *92*

Ideas for Counselors: How to Use This

Book *98*

What Else Can I Read? *101*

Who Can I Call for Help? *103*

Notes *105*

Acknowledgments

I would like to thank the following people, without whom this book never would have happened: Susan, Debbie, Cindy, Jeanne and my critique group, for your caring, encouragement, input and advice; Sabine, Sharon and Sherry for giving of your time, resources and expertise; the teens and mothers of teens who, with tears and sometimes laughter, shared their experiences in order to help others. Last but not least, I would like to thank my editor, Cynthia Bunch-Hotaling, for her patience, advice and expert handholding. May God richly bless you all.

A Letter from the Author

Dear Reader,

If you are young, unmarried and pregnant, or know someone who is, I wrote this book to help you. It's a book about options. It will not tell you what choices to make. It will give you the information you need to make well-thought-out decisions. At the end of each chapter are questions you can use as tools to help you make the choices that fit your unique situation.

You can read *What Now?* on your own, but I would encourage you to read it with a parent, counselor or other supportive adult. You may need help doing some of the exercises. A supportive adult can be your sounding board or your own private Internet, listening and pointing you in the right direction.

I married young and became a mother at age eighteen. Now I am both a mother and a grandmother. While I am not a professional counselor or teacher, I have both counseled and taught. I am a writer, and I love children of all ages.

A few years ago I became involved with teens and their babies in a high-school teen parent program. They were kids just like you, with the same fears and the same options. The majority of them made the courageous choice to carry their babies to term. This

is a decision-making guide for girls like them—and
girls like you.

Now let me introduce you to some other girls who
were in the same situation as you.

Jenna, age 15: "When I found out I was pregnant, I
panicked!"

Cassie, age 17: "*I thought* if I ignored the problem it
would go away."

Krista, age 13: "I didn't know what was wrong at first."

> *Pregnancy is a natural consequence of a natural act. Your baby is not a punishment for premarital sex.*

Melissa, age 14: "How could this happen to me?"

Nichole, age 15: "I didn't want to deal with it at first.
Then I thought, *Now we can get married.*"

None of these girls expected to get pregnant. They
were all confused, angry, scared, frustrated, hurt
and felt very much alone. Can you identify with any
of these feelings?

"God hates me."

"My parents will hate me."

"It's not fair!"

First of all, please realize these feelings are normal.
They are a natural response to any crisis situation.
But feelings are not always grounded in truth. God
does not hate you. And very likely your parents will
not hate you either.

God hates sin, but you and your baby are created
in his image. He loves both of you. God is also in the
business of forgiveness. We call it grace. He will not
take away the consequences of your behavior, but he

wants to walk with you through the hard times to come.

Before we go any further, let's ask one very important question: Are you sure you are really pregnant?

Okay, so your breasts hurt, your stomach rebels at the thought of food, and your period is three days late. Have you had a pregnancy test?

Krista was thirteen when she started feeling sick. She thought she had the flu: *I didn't know what was wrong at first. My girlfriend said, "What if you're pregnant?" So we bought a home pregnancy kit. When the test was positive, I still didn't want to believe it.*

Cassie tried to ignore her symptoms: *I wouldn't let myself even think about the possibility of being pregnant. I didn't want to deal with it for a long time. Then I realized if I didn't make some decisions, someone else would make them for me. This was something that would affect the rest of my life.*

> There is a high incidence of false positive results with some home pregnancy tests.

When Krista's home test was positive, she knew she had to tell her mother: *I was really scared. My best friend went with me. Mom was really mad. When she calmed down, she took me to the doctor. It was true. I was really pregnant. I just sat there and bawled. I didn't know what to do next. This wasn't suppose to happen. Not to me!*

You may be pregnant if you have had sexual intercourse (once counts) and any of these statements are true about you: (1) you have missed a period, (2) your breasts are sore and swollen, (3) you have to urinate frequently, (4) you feel nauseated part or all of the time.

If you have any of these symptoms, go to a doctor or crisis pregnancy center for a pregnancy test. It is simple and painless.

Being unmarried and pregnant is frightening. This book will take you step by step and help you answer the question every girl in your situation asks: "What am I going to do now?"

In Christian love,
Linda Shands

1

....

What Am I Going to Do?

You may think this can't be happen-ing to you. But it is. And wishing won't make it go away. No matter what your circumstances, if you are pregnant, you have some decisions to make.

How Can I Tell My Parents?

If you have not yet told your parents, do it now! It won't be easy; they will certainly be hurt and probably angry, but they have to know.

Jenna was fifteen when she got pregnant. Her parents were divorced, and her father had recently died in an auto accident. She and her mother had just moved to a small town a few miles from where she had grown up.

Jenna remembers: *The first person I told was my mother. She held me and we cried together. She didn't want to believe it, but when we found out for sure, she was really supportive.*

Melissa told her mother first, but neither of them were comfortable telling her father. She says: *Labor was a breeze compared to telling my dad I was pregnant at fourteen. My mom knew right away. Like the day I found out I told her. She was not okay with it, but was going to deal with it. Both of us were afraid if I told my dad he would kick me out of the house. I was like five months pregnant when I finally told him. That was absolutely the worse day of my life.*

He got really upset and said, "Well, obviously you can't have an abortion because you're too far along." That was one of the reasons I waited so long, because I knew he would pressure me in that direction. Abortion—I just couldn't do it. I don't think I could live with myself afterwards.

Melissa's father agreed to let her live at home and offered continued financial support so she could stay in school. She also enrolled in the teen parent program at her school, where teachers and counselors were willing and ready to help.

Who's on My Side?

Cassie and her boyfriend, Steve, were seniors in high school. They had talked about getting married after college. Neither of them was ready for a baby. When they discovered she was pregnant, they found many people were willing and able to help.

Cassie says: *At first I thought if I ignored the problem it would go away. When I finally told my parents, they were upset and wanted to put the blame on someone.*

After the initial shock, both our families and most of our friends were very supportive. They all let us know they would be with us no matter what we decided. One friend from my church youth group put all of her energy into taking care of me. She became a very important part of my life.

My pastor's wife was encouraging. She showed me Scripture verses that related to sin, forgiveness and God's love for me. She also helped me see that my being pregnant was not a sin but a consequence of my sinful actions.

Jenna's mother stuck by her from the start. Jenna soon found that while some people rejected her, others would go out of their way to help.

Jenna says: *When I found out I was pregnant, I panicked. My first reaction was to get an abortion. I had just made the varsity cheerleading squad, and was doing really well in school.*

The father of the baby was older. He was pressuring me to get an abortion. It was like the only choice I had, so I made the appointment. It was a lot harder than I thought it would be.

The church I had grown up in kicked me out because I was considering an abortion. I was not allowed to see my best friend. That made me angry and I wanted to get an abortion even more.

When Jenna's mother wanted to call the pastor's wife at their new community church, Jenna agreed to talk to her: *I told her what had happened. She listened to me and said she had been through the same thing. She knew the kind of hurt I was going through. She said God would always love me and so would she. She promised to be there for me, but I needed information on what I was getting myself into. I wanted to know what my choices were.*

At ten o'clock at night, she found out who was in charge of the crisis pregnancy center and had it opened for me. I got pamphlets on abortion and I read what they would do. I decided that I could not do that to my baby. I had made my choice to sleep with my boyfriend. I could not kill a baby. It was not its fault.

My mom told me, "Honey, make a list of the pros and the cons." When I finished I showed her the list and said, "Mama, as far as I can tell, my baby would die because I want to be a cheerleader."

That's horrible. I knew what the consequences were when I was getting into them. I had made my own choice and I could not make my baby die for my mistake. So I decided no abortion.

A lot of people came up to me and said, "I had an abortion and it's haunted me all of my life." I think that helped me to believe I'd made the right choice. At this point I was about three months pregnant, trying to decide what to do next.

SEE YOUR BABY THROUGH GOD'S EYES
Psalm 139
Jeremiah 1:4-5
Matthew 18:1-5
Exodus 20:13

What Are My Options?

Everyone had their own opinion about what Jenna

should do. Finally her mother suggested she investigate all of the options. Jenna agreed: *That way when people came to me with their opinions I could say, "I have looked into that and it's not the option for me."*

> In one U.S. state, children of teen parents live in poverty five times more often than children born to older parents.[1]

Jenna knew she could not marry the baby's father. She could keep the baby and raise it with her mother's help, but their budget was already tight. Her mother had to work full-time to support the two of them. Jenna had to ask herself, *How can we support a baby? Who will take care of it while we're at school and work?*

I read all the material and came to the conclusion that maybe adoption wouldn't be such a bad thing, so I talked to a lady at an adoption agency. But she made me feel that adoption was my only choice. I was real angry.

Then Mom bought me a crib. She said, "We can keep the baby. We can do this together, no matter what." When she bought me the crib I said, "Whoa, am I ready for this?"

I wanted to be informed. I wanted to do the best thing for my baby. I talk to other girls and they aren't like that at all. They just say, "Of course I'd keep the baby. Of course I wouldn't look into anything else." But if they were pregnant I would tell them, "Just be open-minded. Take advice from everybody then use what you can."

As you can see, the choices were not easy for

Jenna. At fifteen, she was still learning decision-making skills, but she had the wisdom to listen to adults who loved her, as well as her friends. She was mature enough to discover her options, gather information, and make some hard decisions. That took courage.

Who Should I Listen To?

Cassie's choices were not easy ones either: *My parents thought I should keep the baby from the start. Steve wanted to put the baby up for adoption because we both had plans that would be hard to achieve with a baby. His parents agreed. They felt a baby would ruin his future.*

> **OPTIONS**
> ■ Raise your baby yourself, with or without your parents' help.
> ■ Marry your baby's father and raise the baby together.
> ■ Place your baby in an adoptive home.

I went to a Christian unwed mothers' pregnancy center. They gave me information about adoption and raising a child. I talked with a counselor about what our future would be like if I decided to keep our baby or put her up for adoption. Then Steve and I talked and listened to the opinions of our families. We saw that keeping our baby would be the best answer for us.

The first thing I would tell teens to do is seek out a Christian trained in counseling. This person will not tell you what you should do, but will help you see yourself and reality more clearly. Then you can think about your decisions.

Your support group is important too. It's hard to raise a child without people to lean on and get wisdom from, even when two parents are around. Talk to those around you and see how committed to you and the baby they will really be.

> From conception your baby is a living person. By the time you know you are pregnant, your baby has a beating heart, a brain and the beginning of arms and legs.

Always put the child first. A baby is so vulnerable. Decisions should be made with what's best for the baby in mind.

When Jenna and Cassie each realized they carried new life inside them, they made decisions based on what was best for them and their babies.

Reality Check

What about you? First, let's look at your situation. In a separate notebook or on a sheet of paper, answer the following questions. This information is for you, so add your own thoughts or explanations.

1. Where are you living right now?
2. Can you stay there throughout the pregnancy?
3. Who can you count on for emotional support? List everyone who will stand by you.

Cassie's list	*Jenna's list*
Steve	Mother
My parents	Pastor's wife
His parents	Adult friend
Pastor's wife	Teacher
Youth group friend	Some friends
Counselor	
Other friends	

4. Who can you count on for financial support?

Cassie	*Jenna*
Self	Mother
Steve	
Parents	

5. What are your plans for the next three to five years?

6. List any questions, fears and specific needs you have.

Feeling overwhelmed? Take a minute to relax. Talk to God about the things you have listed above. Ask him to help you make the best choices possible for you and your baby. Then share your concerns with someone on your emotional support list. Don't try to tough it out alone.

If you need someone to talk to, a place to live or financial help, see "Who Can I Call for Help?" on page 103.

2

....

What Is
It Like
to Have
a Baby?

*There is a miracle happening in-*side you. Arms and legs are forming, as well as tiny hands and feet, fingers, toes, a beating heart—a miniature human being.

God designed your body to shelter, protect and nourish new life until brain cells are fully formed and tiny lungs can function on their own. Pretty awesome when you think about it.

What Does Being Pregnant Feel Like?
Your body is changing. Hormones that once were your friends now seem as if they are out to get you. Chances are you feel sick sometimes. Your breasts

hurt and will increase in size. You may feel hungry more often than usual, and may crave certain foods.

These physical changes are normal. Your doctor or midwife will help you with any medical or nutritional needs and will monitor your baby's health. At this point, choosing to stay healthy and keep your baby healthy is the most important decision you can make.

If you have not done so already, make a doctor's appointment now.

If you are not sure whom to see, ask someone on your support list to help you.

> *Babies born to teen mothers tend to have a higher incidence of birth defects. Many of these problems can be avoided with good prenatal care.*

As your baby grows, so will you. Pretty soon you will be able to feel him move. Fists and knees and elbows will flutter, poke and push. Your stomach will ripple as he turns over and jump when he gets the hiccups.

Your body is no longer yours alone. Just eat something that disagrees with your baby and watch her tell you about it! Get upset and so will she. Sit quietly and you may feel how she responds to your voice, different kinds of music, a gentle pat, a loving touch.

What Will Labor Be Like?
Let's face it, labor and delivery are hard work. Even the shortest, least complicated vaginal births are painful. But modern methods of delivery are aided by special techniques and breathing exercises that make giving birth easier.

In a recent segment of her comic strip, *For Better or for Worse*, Lynn Johnston shows a young pregnant woman asking questions of an older, more experienced mother. When the young woman admits she is afraid of the pain, the older mother tells her, "You don't think about the pain when you're producing a miracle."[2]

> DO YOU . . .
> ■ smoke tobacco?
> ■ drink liquor, beer or wine?
> ■ smoke marijuana?
> ■ do any other drugs?
> If you answered yes to any of these questions, please discuss them with your doctor. *Your life and the life of your baby may depend on it.*

You will probably hear all kinds of stories, from tales of horror to "It was no big deal." But like your baby, each birth is unique. What was true for someone else may not be true for you.

Your doctor or midwife is the one most qualified to guide you through both pregnancy and delivery. He or she will tell you what to expect, and probably recommend childbirth classes and a tour of the hospital or clinic.

What If I Decide to Keep My Baby?

The wonders of carrying new life inside you will not change the fact that you are young and unmarried with an uncertain future. In a few short months, your baby will be born. He or she will still need nurturing, protection, food, clothing and shelter.

> *Taking care of someone else's child is much different from having full charge of your own.*

Krista remembers: *I never thought about not keep-*

ing Andy. My school had a teen parent program. They talked a lot about how to eat right and take care of my body. They offered us counseling, and the people at Adult and Family Services gave us money and rides to the doctor.

We were supposed to learn how to take care of a baby, but I thought, "Big deal. You feed them and diaper them. What's so hard about that?" I used to baby-sit my nephew a lot.

The day I brought Andy home he wet the crib sheet three times. He spit up when I fed him and cried when I put him down. I thought babies slept all the time. Boy, was I wrong.

He was so cute! When he started smiling, I wanted to play with him all day. But I had to go to school. He got sick a lot too. Sometimes my mom would help out, but she worked and so did my stepdad. It was pretty much up to me.

Andy was born in July. I planned to go back to school in September just like normal. But it didn't work like that. Most mornings I was just too tired to get up. Andy had his days and nights switched around. When I did take him to the daycare center at school, he slept all day for them, then cried all night.

What Will It Be Like to Take Care of an Infant?

Babies are sweet, soft, innocent and helpless. They need someone to feed and change them. They also need love and attention to survive. They learn by listening as we talk or sing to them, watching our facial expressions and feeling our touch.

For a while Jenna imagined her only responsible

choice would be to parent her baby. She thought a lot about the baby's birth and how she would take care of him.

I was an only child and didn't know much about baby care or an infant's needs. Of course, I thought I could do it with no problem.

I have a friend who has a daughter my age and had just had another baby. She was older and a stay-at-home mom. She was married and happy, and she still said, "Jenna, it is hard!"

She told me she saw a talk show on TV where the lady was so tired, and the baby was colicky and wouldn't stop crying, so she stuck him in the

> **Your baby is helpless. He depends on you to take care of him.**

freezer and went and took a nap, then woke up and realized what she had done.

My friend said, "I could see how someone could get to that point."

When a grown woman who's already been a mother and has no stress at all is telling me she could see how this could happen, I thought, how could a fifteen-year-old who is going to school be okay?

The adults in my life had been right so far. When they told me what having a baby was all about and said that parenting was going to be a struggle, I decided I'd better believe them.

I think teenagers need to just cut the pride and look at what adults are saying. All my friends were just, "Oh, it's going to be so cute," but they're not around at three o'clock in the morning.

Remember that your baby is helpless. He depends on you to take care of him. Right now, while you are pregnant, you can do that by staying away from cigarettes, drugs and alcohol, eating right and getting good prenatal care. Then decide if you can meet the needs of your child as he grows and changes after birth.

Krista says: *I thought being a mom would come naturally, that I'd automatically know what to do. But after Andy was born I was scared to hold him. He was so tiny. The first time I bathed him, he turned blue. I grabbed him and ran to the neighbor's. She checked him all over and told me he was just cold, and to make sure the bathroom was warmer next time.*

Let's take a look at some facts about babies and what caring for one is really like.

An Infant . . .	Teen Moms Say . . .
Is cute and cuddly.	"He's fun to hold and show off to my friends."
Needs constant attention.	"I can't leave her even for a minute."
Needs to be cuddled, talked to, played with and loved.	"I don't have time to hold him."
	"I love her, but sometimes I get bored."
Picks up on Mom's stress.	"I get up, feed and change the baby, do a load of laundry, go to school, come home and start all over again. There's no time for me!"

An Infant . . .	Teen Moms Say . . .
Cries more when Mom's upset.	"I'm so tired. It seems like all I do is yell at him. He's just a baby. He doesn't understand."
Cries for no apparent reason.	"I worry all the time: Is she sick? Hungry? What's wrong with her?"
Sleeps only when you cannot.	"I'm exhausted, but I have to get my homework done."
Spits up, runs fevers, ear infections.	"I just took him to the gets doctor. He can't be sick again!"
Costs money.	"I had to buy diapers and formula. Now I'm broke."

Will I Ever Have a Life?

Krista finally transferred to a community college where she could earn her GED (general equivalency diploma), giving her the same status as a high-school graduate. The schedule was not quite so demanding, but there were other problems: *I had to take the city bus, and everyone would look at me, then look at Andy, and shake their heads. I knew they were thinking "Poor little baby," and it made me mad.*

I really missed my friends. When I'd see them they'd say, "You can't ever go anywhere, so why should we call?" And most of the boys were jerks—all friendly until they found out I wouldn't sleep with them. Then they're history.

Sometimes when I really needed a break, I'd take

Andy to my sister's and just go home and sleep.

Krista remembers telling a friend: *When I'm eighteen, Andy will be four years old. I want him to have a life. I want me to have a life! I'm doing the best I can, but I worry that it's not enough.*

We will hear more about Krista later. For now, let's get back to you. Are you really ready to be a mother? Do you have the physical, emotional and financial resources to meet your child's needs, even when you must sacrifice your own? Are you willing to commit the next eighteen years of your life to raising this child?

FANTASIES AND FACTS
FANTASY: Parenting will be fun.
FACT: Parenting is sometimes fun. More often it is hard, unrewarding, repetitive work. Ask any parent.
FANTASY: I can work, go to school, be a single parent and still have time for a social life.
FACT: You will work at home, at school, at a part-time job and be too exhausted for a social life. Ask any single parent.
FANTASY: My friends will be around all the time after the baby is born. Nothing will change.
FACT: Your friends will be busy with sports and boys. Your world will revolve around your child.

What Can I Expect As My Baby Gets Older?

We are jumping ahead here, but to understand what parenting a baby is really like, we need to look beyond the infancy stage.

As Krista found out, a baby grows up fast. As he changes, so do his needs: *In some ways it was easier when Andy got a little older. He slept all night and usually took a nap. He didn't need to be changed as much. He could point to things and say words to tell me what he wanted. Like a real little person, you know?*

But he was into everything. He wouldn't always come when I called him. If I took him to the store he'd grab something off the shelf and then scream when I took it away from him. It was so embarrassing. I felt like a bad mom. I didn't know what to do.

At five to six months your baby will sit up on her own and crawl. Around a year, she will learn to walk. She will take your hand and lead you where she wants to go. She will give neck-squeezing hugs and slobbery wet kisses. When you sit, she will want to sit on your lap. When you are trying to study she will want a story. She will want you at naptime and bedtime, but really won't want to sleep at all.

A Toddler . . .	**Teen Moms Say . . .**
Is cute, curious and active.	"He's fun to play with."
	"He won't sit still!"
Demands constant attention.	"I can't even go to the bathroom alone."
Needs protection.	"She grabbed a knife off the kitchen counter. I didn't know she could reach that high!"
Is rebellious and self-centered.	"Why can't he be good?"
Needs teaching and direction.	"She won't eat for me."
	"He's doing that on purpose!"
	"She doesn't listen."
Needs vaccines, vitamins, proper nutrition, shoes and clothing.	
Throws up, falls down, eats cat food, flushes toys down the toilet.	

Krista says: *When Andy was eighteen months old, he followed me into the bathroom all the time. Usually he just unrolled*

> **Ninety percent of parenting a toddler is teaching right from wrong. Discipline (not punishment) requires time, energy and consistency.**

the toilet paper, but one night he flushed one of those little cars down the toilet. My landlord had to take the whole thing apart.

Another time he climbed to the top of the linen closet and found a bottle of sleeping pills. It had one of those childproof caps, you know? But he got it open anyway. We had to rush him to the emergency center and get his stomach pumped.

Reality Check

Let's look ahead and see what it would be like to bring a baby into your living situation.

1. Keep track of your time for a week. Use this information to make a schedule. Your weekday schedule might look something like this:

Monday-Friday

7:00 a.m.   Shower, dress, do hair and makeup, grab a yogurt

7:30   Ride bus to school

8:00   Begin school

3:00 p.m.   Ride bus home after school ends

3:30   Hang with friends, watch TV, do chores

6:00   Eat dinner

6:30   Do homework

8:00 Watch TV
10:00 Go to bed

Include the weekend, since Saturday and Sunday will have different routines.

2. Get out the phone book. Determine what local resources are available to help you after your baby is born. Examples: (1) Birth to Three provides support and information on baby care. (2) Through the federal government's special supplemental food program for Women, Infants and Children (WIC), qualified mothers can obtain vouchers to purchase food for themselves and their babies.

> **A TODDLER'S PROPERTY LAWS**
> 1. If I like it, it's mine.
> 2. If it's in my hand, it's mine.
> 3. If I can take it away from you, it's mine.
> 4. If I had it a little while ago, it's mine.
> 5. If it's mine, it must never appear to be yours in any way.
> 6. If I'm doing or building something, all the pieces are mine.
> 7. If it looks like mine, it's mine.
> 8. If I saw it first, it's mine.
> 9. If you are playing with something and you put it down, it automatically becomes mine.
> 10. If it's broken, it's yours.[3]

3. Read at least one book on child care (see "What Else Can I Read?" on page 101).

4. Take the schedule you made in step one. Decide where a baby will fit in: bath, feeding, changing, packing his bag for day care, as well as time for play, extra shopping and laundry.

Your new schedule might look something like this:

Monday-Friday
5:30 a.m. Throw pillow at alarm
5:35 Throw last night's wash into dryer
5:45 Change and feed baby
6:10 Mix formula, locate pacifier, pack diaper bag
6:30 Hunt through dryer for clean sleepers and socks

6:40 Change and dress baby

7:00 Shower, dress, do hair and makeup, grab a yogurt

7:30 Drop baby off at daycare center

8:00 Begin school

If you are sure your toddler cannot reach, open, or otherwise get into something harmful, think again.

12:00 noon. Call to check on baby, run to store for diapers, use pay phone to set up doctor's appointment, gobble down banana and granola bar

3:00 Pick up baby

3:30 Arrive home

3:35 Feed, change, cuddle and play with baby

4:30 Pray the baby sleeps a while, grab a sandwich, do necessary personal or household chores

6:30 Eat dinner

6:35 Feed, bathe and change screaming baby

8:00 Fall asleep over homework with baby on your chest

10:00 Feed and change baby

10:30 Throw load of laundry in washer

10:40 Sneak into bed

1:30 a.m. Change, feed and play with baby, or walk the floor if she's fussy

3:30 Sneak back into bed

5:30 Throw pillow at alarm

Weekends: Instead of school do shopping, errands and cleaning.

3

....

What Will
Having a
Baby Cost?

Krista had some things to learn
about caring for her baby's physical needs. And,
because she did not plan ahead, she also had some
unpleasant surprises.

*When I was growing up, I never thought much
about money. We weren't rich, but my mom and
stepdad
pretty much
took care of
food and
clothes and*

**By reading this book and doing the
research and activities at the end of each
chapter, you are planning ahead.**

*things like that. I spent my allowance on CDs and
earrings. When Andy was born all that changed. I*

*had to help buy formula and diapers. My stepdad
paid for the doctor and hospital. I think insurance
helped some.*

Who Will Pay My Medical Bills?
Because Krista was under nineteen and lived at home,
her parents' insurance covered some of the cost of
her prenatal care and hospital bills.

Krista's pregnancy was routine, and Andy's birth
was normal. The overall fee for prenatal care, delivery
and hospital was $2200. Krista's parents paid twenty
percent, or $440, of that cost. If there had been
complications with her pregnancy or delivery, or if she
or Andy had needed special care, the fee could have
been much higher.

Krista also had to take Andy to the doctor for
immunizations against childhood diseases, well-baby
checkups, ear infections and bronchitis. Before she
went on welfare and got a Medicaid card, this cost her fifteen dollars a visit.

> *If you choose adoption for your child,
> the adoptive family will usually pay your
> hospital and doctor expenses.*

Krista was surprised by how much she
needed to spend: *I never realized before how expensive prescriptions and cough medicine and baby Tylenol are.*

Doctor visits are a given when it comes to raising
a child. But health care for yourself and your baby
is not free. Someone has to pay: you, your parents,
your insurance company or the government.

What Supplies Will I Need?

Each day a baby goes through about ten diapers and two or three changes of clothing. He needs to be fed every two to four hours, nights included, which may require up to eight bottles of formula.

A baby generates at least two extra loads of laundry and one trip to the supermarket per week. The shopping list includes the following:

One-time purchases		Weekly or monthly items
crib	crib sheets	diapers
mattress pad	high chair	lotion
baby bath	bottles	baby cereal
car seat	play pen	diaper rash ointment
sleepers	blankets	baby shampoo
undershirts	pacifier	formula
rattles	toys	
baby spoon	teething ring	
toddler cup		

If you choose to breast-feed, you will need a breast pump for those times when you are at school or work, and someone other than you is caring for your baby.

Caution: Do not skimp on the crib. Doctors warn that an infant should sleep on his back or side, on a smooth, firm surface. Putting a newborn to sleep on a pile of soft blankets, bean-bag chair or

Secondhand stores are good sources for clothes and toys.

water bed could cause the baby to smother.

Will I Have to Work?

This depends on your age and your living circumstances. Are your parents willing and able to support you and a baby? Do you qualify for government assistance?

When Krista moved in with her boyfriend, she had to rely on welfare to support them. To receive her welfare check, the law said she had to stay in school.

Lots of times Andy was sick and I had to stay home with him. I could never get my homework done, so I failed most of my classes.

Not only did Krista need the financial assistance she received from the state while going to school, but she needed that high-school diploma.

For a while I went to school and worked afternoons, but I had to quit. I didn't want to stay on welfare all my life, but I sure couldn't support us on what I made at the fast-food place.

We will cover government financial assistance in more detail in chapter six.

Will I Have to Pay for Child Care?

Again, that depends on your circumstances. Many high schools now offer infant and toddler care. In some cases the government pays the fees. In others you are responsible for some or all of the cost.

Depending on where you live, qualified child care can run anywhere from three hundred to five hundred dollars a month. Even if a relative or friend is willing to watch your baby, there may be costs involved.

Reality Check

Let's take a closer look at your financial situation:[4]

1. Are you covered by medical insurance? If so, how much of your pregnancy, delivery and hospital cost will it pay? How much will it pay for well-baby checkups, shots, medication, etc.?

2. Visit a grocery store, discount store and some garage sales to determine the costs of the following items: crib, dresser, bassinet, bottles, car seat, high chair, diapers, wipes, baby food, formula, diaper rash ointment.

3. Call local doctors or pediatricians and research the cost of well-baby visits, immunizations and visits for colds, flu and ear infections.

4. Call or visit a pharmacy and research the cost of antibiotics, children's Tylenol, children's cough syrup and a rectal or ear thermometer.

If you decide to parent your baby, you will need this list to complete your budget.

5. What jobs will you qualify for after you graduate from high school? Call employers or look in the help wanted section of your newspaper to determine the pay rates for those jobs. How many of these jobs are actually available?

Examples:

Fast-food restaurant worker	$5.50/hour
Department store clerk	$6.00/hour
Receptionist	$6.50/hour
Data entry clerk	$6.50/hour

6. Call or visit several daycare centers. Ask the following questions:

a. What services do they provide?

b. Do they take infants?

c. Are infants and toddlers in separate rooms?

d. Do they hold and play with the baby, as well as meet his physical needs?

e. Do they supply food and/or diapers?

f. What are their hours? (If they are open from 8:00 a.m. to 6:00 p.m. and you are at school and work from 8:00 to 7:00, that center would not be a good choice.)

g. What do they charge? (If you bring home $600 a month and the center charges $400 a month, you should probably look elsewhere.)

h. Will they accept a government subsidy?

7. Look in your local paper. Call people who offer in-home child care and ask the following questions:

a. What services do they provide?

b. What are their hours?

c. What do they charge?

8. If a relative has offered to baby-sit, find out the following:

a. What days and hours are they available?

b. Do these days and hours coincide with your schedule, or will you use this relative only in an emergency?

c. How will they charge? Figure the cost of food and supplies you must provide. (Melissa's aunt watched her baby for free, but Melissa provided all the food, formula and diapers.)

This may seem like a lot of work. But it's better to know the answers now than face unpleasant surprises later.

4

....

What About
My Baby's
Father?

From the beginning God planned for man and woman to become one. Together they were to shelter, nourish and provide for each new life created. But it has not always worked out that way.

The father of Jenna's baby was older and already out of school, but his reaction to the news that she was pregnant convinced her that she did not want him to be a part of her or her baby's life: *I told my boyfriend I was pregnant as soon as I found out for sure. I went to his house that night. He told me, "You've got to leave. I'll call you later; I'm having people over," and shut the door in my face.*

He called me later and his reaction was, "What's

going on? You'll get an abortion. I don't want anything to do with it." He never offered any support. I had to fight to get him to agree to pay for the abortion and give me a ride to the clinic. It took a lot of threatening.

When Jenna decided not to go through with the abortion, she never heard from the baby's father again.

I found out later the person coming over that night was his fiancée. He was engaged the whole time and I never knew anything about it. Boy, did I feel stupid.

Is He Ready to Be a Father?

The dictionary defines a father as a male who has begotten a child, a male parent. The Bible says a father's role is to provide for his children, protect them, discipline them in love, teach and train them in the way they should go. He is to set an example, be responsible for them and accountable to God for the way he raises them. Wow! That's quite a responsibility.

Think about the young man whose child is growing

In Oregon, only 39 percent of boys who get a girl pregnant graduate from high school.[5]

inside you. Okay, so maybe you would rather not, but do it anyway. Who is he? I don't mean Jimmy Johnson, a senior at Melrose High. I mean who is he on the inside, where it really counts?

Does he accept responsibility? Not just for the life he helped create, but for other things as well. If he skips school or cannot keep a job, chances are he won't be able to stick it out through nine months of pregnancy and the birth of a baby, let alone the eighteen years it will take to bring the child up.

Does he make promises and keep them? Is he honest or deceitful? Abusive or kind? Has he ever hit you, forced you to have sex or hurt you physically in any way?

Will My Boyfriend Stick with Me?

The role your baby's father plays in your life and your baby's life will depend on many factors. If he is still in school, has no income and no idea of what he wants out of life, the chances of his taking an active part in your pregnancy or supporting the baby are slim.

Melissa's boyfriend was supportive at first, but the relationship was severed a few months after their daughter Kaylee was born: *Travis was around—if you want to call it around. Especially through the first two trimesters he was there for me to confide in. He and I split up for good when Kaylee was three months old. It was a rocky relationship from the start. He had another girl. He got into drugs and alcohol. I didn't want any part of that.*

Last May he called to wish me happy Mother's Day. I was surprised. His dad brought me a little bit of money once. Kaylee doesn't know Travis is her father. She's too young to understand.

What Are the Father's Rights?

If your baby's father does decide to take an active role, ask yourself how much you want him to be involved. Can he help with financial support? Will he stick by you when things get tough?

Yes, he is just as responsible as you are for conceiving the baby. But you are the one who will shelter and nourish the child with your body. You are the one who will give birth. You must be the one to dictate his place in the decision-making process.

While it is true that a father's name on a birth certificate can force him to pay child support if he has the means, it may also give him, and possibly his family, custody and visiting rights unless otherwise worked out in court.

When Andy was a few months old, Krista's boyfriend begged her to move in with him: *He swore he loved me. But after two months I knew it wasn't going to work. He wouldn't even look for a job. My*

> New welfare laws require you to identify the father of your child.

caseworker didn't know it, but we were living off my welfare checks. When I tried to leave, he and his family threatened to file for custody of the baby.

Krista was terrified. She had no idea what her rights were, let alone his: *Even though he didn't do anything to support us, the judge awarded him and his family visiting rights.*

Because his name was on the birth certificate as the baby's father, Krista had no choice but to go along with the court's decision.

Should We Get Married?

That depends. For Jenna, Melissa and Krista, the answer was a definite no. Nichole and Jerry immediately said yes, and later regretted it. Cassie and

Steve took time to think it out. Their relationship worked because they worked at their relationship.

Your decision to marry the baby's father will depend on a lot of things. Do you love each other? Are you willing to make a commitment to each other and the child you will raise? Are you willing to work hard and make the sacrifices necessary to see it through? Will your combined incomes allow you to support your child?

Cassie and Steve's situation proves that getting married is not necessarily a now or never decision. They both wanted a college education. They also wanted to be good parents to their daughter and establish a solid marriage relationship. With help from their families, they were able to achieve those goals.

Cassie says: *I knew this child would be worth the struggles and sacrifices that would come with her. I also knew that I had matured enough and had the character qualities necessary to be a good parent.*

When we decided not to put Tess up for adoption we also decided to put marriage off for a year. We knew that becoming parents was going to be a big adjustment and decided not to add the stress of starting a marriage at the same time. We felt that we could both develop bonds with Tess and provide her with a good environment even if we weren't married.

That year was hard for us in some ways. Steve attended a state university two hours away. I lived with my parents and attended a small college in our hometown. On weekends, I took the baby and stayed at Steve's parents' home. This allowed Steve to take

*care of her and really get to know what being a father
was like.*

*I think waiting a year had a positive effect on our
marriage. We were much more confident of our commitment to each other and our ability to parent. There
were obviously stressful times, but we were both
striving for the same goals, the most important being
Tess, and were able to work together well.*

**YOU CAN HAVE A
SUCCESSFUL MARRIAGE
IF . . .**
■ **you are best friends as
well as lovers.**
■ **you are committed to
each other.**
■ **your marriage is
committed to God.**
■ **you are both willing to
work at your relationship.**
■ **the word *divorce* is not
in your vocabulary.**

---

*Every child deserves two
parents. Every mom needs
someone to share the responsibilities. Raising a child is a
very serious and stressful
commitment that works much
better when two caring parents are involved.*

There was a time when cou-
ples involved in premarital sex
were forced to marry, espe-
cially when a baby was involved. But pregnancy
should never be the main reason for marriage. Nothing cools a hot love faster than a pile of unpaid bills,
a screaming infant and an exhausted wife. There are
few young men mature enough to sacrifice their
dreams and take up the cross of marital and parental
responsibility.

Even if he truly wants to offer his child love and
support, the problems may be insurmountable. Can
he finish high school, hold down a job, stay faithful,
support a wife and baby?

Nichole and Jerry decided the answers were yes.
They were married shortly after their baby was born,

halfway through their junior year: *I thought it would be kind of romantic, you know? We'd have our own apartment. We could be together every night. I'd decorate the nursery with all my stuffed animals.*

It was okay at first. We went to classes during the day, while Benjamin stayed at the school's daycare center. Then Jerry worked at a grocery store from 4:00 to midnight. Our parents still had to help us pay the rent, but we were getting by—until I got pregnant again.

I was so sick. Jerry had to stay home and take care of Benjamin. Neither of us was going to

> **Half of all abused children have teen parents.**

school. Then he lost his job. He was really angry. He started spanking Ben just because he cried. Once he threw him into the wall. Then he hit me in the stomach and I almost lost the baby.

It really scared me. I told him he would have to leave. But he wouldn't. He said it was his home, his wife and his children and he could do whatever he wanted to us.

With her mother's help, Nichole finally went to court and filed a restraining order against Jerry. Rather than continue paying rent on a two-bedroom apartment, her parents told Nichole she could move back in with them.

In spite of the problems, marriage may sometimes be the right answer. Having two parents who love and support each other is certainly the best for any baby.

Reality Check

1. If you are thinking of marrying the father of your

child, please take another look at some of the questions from the beginning of this chapter:

    a. Does he accept responsibility in all areas of his life?

    b. Does he keep his promises? Not just to you, but to his parents, teachers and friends.

    c. Is he honest, or does he sometimes tell a fib to get out of a sticky situation? Does he ever lie about where he is going or where he has been?

    d. Has he ever hit you or anyone else?

    e. Has he ever forced you to have sex?

2. Go back to the Reality Check in chapter three and evaluate the answers to those questions together. How will your financial and child-care situations change if you are married?

3. Get the best premarital counseling available. Even if you were not pregnant, most pastors require premarital counseling before they will perform a wedding. Marriage is work. (Trust me. I have

> *If he hits you,* **leave.** *There is* **never** *a reason to stay in an abusive situation.*

been at it for more than thirty years.) Turning two into one is not an easy task. Add number three, a baby, into the equation and the result can be total chaos.

5

....

Should I Live with My Parents?

If you have decided that marrying the baby's father is not an option right now, you have some quick decisions to make. Where will you go? How will you live?

Some girls who do not have parental support live with other relatives, with friends or in shelters for pregnant women. Most girls live at home for a while, at least throughout the pregnancy. But what about after the baby is born?

Jenna released her baby to his adoptive parents the day after he was born. But Krista, Melissa, Nichole and Cassie all lived with their infants in their parents' homes for a period of time. If living at home is an option for you, it is important to remember that your relationship with your parents will change.

How Will My Relationship with My Parents Change?

Melissa's mother allowed her to stay at home and helped her break the news of her pregnancy to her father. But their idea of what Melissa should do was completely different from her own: *When my father realized I was too far along for an abortion, they really pushed me in the direction of adoption. They set up an appointment with someone at an adoption agency. I never did go.*

After Kaylee was born, Melissa and her parents still struggled with their new relationship: *The hard part is you're still the child. I mean, you have a child, but you still have to do what Mom and Dad say.*

No matter how much your parents love you and want to help, there is bound to be conflict. Think about it. You have been their child for thirteen, fourteen or fifteen years. Now even though you are suddenly a mother yourself, they cannot just flip the parent switch to off. They can have the best intentions in the world, but their perspectives may not always be the same as yours.

Melissa says: *The worst time I can remember, when Kaylee was an infant, Dad told me to take out the trash and I said okay, but I was still breast-feeding and the baby needed to be fed right then. I said, "Well, you need to wait. I'm feeding the baby." And he said "No, you're going to take out the trash like I told you to. Now!" And I said, "I can't do it now." And he said,*

"I'm the parent here. I told you to do your chores."

I remember this so clearly. I absolutely wanted to kill him. You know your hormones after you have a baby; you're right up there and ready to explode anyway. It was just awful. In fact I threatened to just leave right then. I basically told him I was going to finish feeding Kaylee and when I was done and laid her down I would take out the trash.

That was our first and biggest power struggle after the baby was born. It got better after that. I did do my chores, but it was hard. Now looking back on that, even though I can't agree with what he did, I can see how hard it would be: he still was the parent, I was still living under that roof.

What Melissa did not realize at the time was that although her father loved her, he still thought of her as his child. Among other things, he was dealing with his own guilt, hurt feelings and anger that his daughter should be in this situation. Once they talked it out he admitted he should have been more patient, and Melissa agreed to be more respectful.

How Will My Relationship with My Siblings Change?

Melissa says: *My sister was thirteen. She matured a lot through my pregnancy. She went from the snotty little brat to someone I could really trust. I confided in her mostly, because I swear when you get pregnant, you find out who your friends are. If you don't want to party or have big fun anymore you really find out. My sister was always there. It was good that she was around. I would have gone insane.*

Living at home affects your siblings as much as it does you and your parents. They may be excited, or angry about having a new baby in the house. Babies take time and energy, something your siblings might be willing to help with, but could just as well resent.

Be sure to include brothers and sisters in your family meetings. Depending on their ages, they may even have a say in some of the decisions.

Who Will Be Responsible for the Baby?

As Kaylee grew, Melissa's father spent more time with the baby. He became an important part of his granddaughter's life. Melissa's mother had been supportive from the start, but Melissa had conflicts with her as well: *I wouldn't leave Kaylee there. If I went to the grocery store, I always wanted to take her. Mom got kind of mad about that because she thought I didn't trust her. It wasn't that I didn't trust her; I think I was just really overprotective.*

> **If you are under eighteen, your parents are still legally responsible for you.**

Melissa did not want to burden her parents with Kaylee's care: *While I was still pregnant I sat down and talked to my mom and dad. I said, "You know this is my baby, and I don't expect you to raise her. If you guys ever feel like you're putting too much into it, then tell me and I'll take up more slack."*

It was tough right after I had her. I didn't have a job for a few months. They bought all the diapers and stuff. I felt like I was indebted to them, like she was their child. When I went to work I got another baby sitter. At school, the Infant Center watched her.

We had a lot of hard times. Then I think, what would it be like if Kaylee grew up and brought her baby home to live with me? And I begin to understand how my parents must have felt. So given the circumstances, I guess it went pretty well. But sometimes, it's really tough to hold your tongue.

In some cases, if you are very young, your parents may feel like they should step in and make decisions for you.

When Krista's boyfriend left for good, her mother encouraged her to come back home. She knew Krista was having a hard time emotionally and in school. She also saw her daughter's struggle to parent Andy and thought her own experience as a mother entitled her to assume that role with her grandson.

Krista remembers: *It was hard on all of us. My mom quit her job and just took over with Andy. It was like he was her baby and I was just her older kid. I was already a mom, but she still wanted me to live by her rules.*

As Krista discovered, parents do not always agree about the role they should play in their daughter's or grandchild's life: *My stepdad said Mom needed to go back to work and I had to shape up and get a job. I couldn't; I was too young. All the jobs went to the older kids. Besides, I had to stay in school. They expected me to act like an adult but treated me like a little kid. We were fighting all the time. When my counselor found me a one-room apartment, I took it.*

How Can I Make It Work?

As you can see by Krista's experience, there are many issues to solve. Practical things such as sleeping arrangements in a crowded home, disrupted routines, new schedules, the extra burden on family finances, child care duties, your continued education. Emotions will play a part on both sides. Guilt, distrust, hurt feelings, disappointment, even anger will have to be dealt with if you are to maintain a family relationship.

> **YOU CAN LIVE PEACEFULLY WITH YOUR PARENTS IF...**
> ■ you work out the details ahead of time on the following: my space/your space, my expectations/your expectations, my responsibilities/your responsibilities.
> ■ everyone is willing to compromise.
> ■ everyone is willing to communicate.
> ■ everyone practices respect.

It may be tempting to ignore your relationship with your parents or take it for granted. Don't! Hold a family conference as soon as possible. Get counseling as a family. No matter how hard it may be, it is necessary to deal with the emotional issues as well as the practical ones.

Are Mom and Dad physically strong enough to help out? Will either parent resent the situation so much that it causes unbearable stress on their relationship? Can they afford to take on the extra expenses of your pregnancy and baby care? Answering these questions now may help avoid conflict in the future.

When Cassie and Steve decided to put off marriage for a year, they met with both families and laid out a plan. Cassie would live at home with her parents and attend the local city college, while Steve began his studies at a state university several miles away.

Cassie tells us: *Family had always been an important part of my life. My parents thought I should keep my baby from the start, and my brothers told me they would help in any way they could.*

That doesn't mean it was always easy. My parents are both professionals. They often went to bed at midnight and got up at six. A baby can play havoc with a good night's sleep. No matter what kind of night we had, they had to go to work the next morning.

I scheduled my school hours so I could be home with Tess in the mornings. She went to a daycare center from eleven until three, when one of my brothers picked her up. I always tried to be home by four. It was a hectic schedule. I often felt bad that except for the small amount of money Steve was able to send, my parents were supporting us. But it was important to them that I finish my education.

On weekends Tess and I stayed at Steve's parents' home so we could be together as a family. It wasn't ideal, but it worked. I know in my heart that without our families' support we could never have made it through that first year.

How Long Should I Live at Home?

Even when everyone involved agrees that it is best for you to live at home for a while, there will come a time when you have to become self-supportive. Cassie's parents helped out for a year after Tess was born. Krista's mother provided a home and financial help for over eighteen months.

Nichole's parents were supportive too. When Jerry

refused to leave their apartment, she moved back into her childhood home. A few months later, her second son was born: *It was pretty crowded. My sister had to sleep on the couch in the family room. She was nice about it; she even offered to keep Benjamin in there with her, but I know it was a pain.*

Mom and Dad said I could stay as long as I needed to, but after Kyle came it was just too much. The cost of formula had almost doubled since Ben was born. Jerry got another job, and my parents thought I should go back to him. They don't believe in divorce. It was like they'd forgotten what he did before, you know?

I said I'd go back if Jerry would get counseling. He started with a counselor at church, then decided to join the navy. They sent our housing allowance straight to me. The kids and I got a two-bedroom apartment and Jerry was hardly ever home. I kept thinking maybe someday he'd get it together. I had to.

Reality Check

If you are thinking of living at home after your baby is born, call a family meeting to discuss the following questions:

1. Where will the baby and I sleep?
2. What changes will my siblings have to make?
3. Who will take care of the baby while I'm at home? At school? At work?
4. What bills or living expenses will I be responsible for?
5. What household chores will I be responsible for?
6. What rules will I be expected to obey?

6

....

Can I
Make It
on My Own?

Melissa decided she wanted a
little more independence, so she moved out of her
parents' home when Kaylee turned one.

*My grandmother had this big house out in the
country. It was too much for her, so she said I could
rent the downstairs. I paid her two hundred dollars a
month. I was working at a department store making
like six-something an hour.*

*I lived out there for two or three months, then moved
into a small apartment with a friend and her little boy.
We split the rent, but we didn't get along very well. It
was hard to live in such a small area. She wasn't
working, so she was there all the time. That was really*

difficult because the kids fought like cats and dogs.
Like siblings, I'm sure. It was awful. It put a lot of
stress on our relationship. That lasted four months,
then she moved out and I moved here with my brother.
The rent is a little more expensive, but I think it's
worth it because the environment is better.

That's really important to me. When Kaylee was
younger and not going outside and stuff, I could live
downtown, anywhere. Now when I look for a place
it's a big deal to me where it's at, what's around and
what kind of people are there. It's a lot more expensive
to find a nice place, but I was afraid for her to go
outside at that other apartment.

How Can I Finish School?

Both Krista and Nichole depended on government
assistance for a while. The hardest part for Krista
was the requirement to finish high school.

If I didn't go to school, I'd lose my money. Besides,
you can't get a job without a high-school diploma. We
had the daycare center at the school, but the kids were
always sick there. Sometimes you just had to stay
home. But you still had to complete school assign-
ments and pass classes if you wanted to graduate.
No graduation, no money.

What About Welfare Benefits?

When Krista went out on her own, welfare paid the
rent on her little apartment. She received food
stamps and had a Medicaid card so she and Andy
could get the care they needed: *I was on welfare for*
over two years before I found out where the money

came from. After Andy left, I got a job. I was really excited about my first paycheck. When I opened it, I thought, "Whoa, they ripped me off!" I mean, I knew they

> **In one state, teen pregnancy costs the public $200 million per year in welfare, medical and other costs.**

took out taxes and stuff, but so much?

My mom just laughed. "Where do you think your welfare checks came from? The government takes money from people who work to pay people who don't work." She said it was no big deal and I should be glad I could get help when I needed it. But I was embarrassed.

As long as Nichole and Jerry were both in school, they received government assistance. They too had food stamps and a Medicaid card. Because he was under eighteen, Jerry's part-time job did not count against the money he received. But when they both dropped out of high school, the welfare payments stopped.

When Jerry and I separated, I thought I could get back on welfare. But they said not while I was married and living with my parents. I was too sick to go back to school. They told me to file for child support. I just laughed. Where would Jerry get any money? He couldn't support us before.

The sad fact is that money available for welfare is running out. Some people abuse the system by taking welfare assistance when they could be working. Laws put in place to stop this abuse may result in money being withheld from people who really need it.

In order to make the best use of funds available, the

government has passed some new laws. A national welfare-reform bill was signed into law by President Clinton in August 1996. If you will need to live on government assistance, many of the changes reflected in this bill will apply to you.

For example, *will you be prepared to have a job within two years?* The new law requires most welfare recipients to find work within that period of time.

> By the time you read this, many of the laws concerning government assistance will have changed both at the state and national level.

Lifetime welfare benefits are now limited to five years. *What would you do if you lost your job and your lifetime benefits ran out?* Each state is allowed to set more rigid limits. *Do you know the time limits in your state?*

Your state now receives a specified amount of money from the federal government. Then the state government officials decide what programs or agencies to spend it on. *Do you know what programs are available in your state and which of those you qualify for?*

Finally, the new law may penalize welfare recipients who do not help establish the paternity of illegitimate children. *Are you able and willing to identify your baby's father?* You may be required to do so in order to receive full welfare benefits.

> Remember that each state has its own programs. Check your phone book, pregnancy center or church office for programs in your state.

How Can I Plan for a Future?

If you plan to go on to college, you will need to decide how to pay for it. Will you have to work? Will the jobs you qualify for fit into a baby-school-work schedule? Can you earn enough to pay for tuition, books and child care?

Melissa is eighteen now. She attends a small community college where she is working on a business degree, and she plans to go on to nursing school: *I always had dreams of going to a big university. When I was fifteen and pregnant, I shoved those dreams in a closet. I was pretty bummed out. But it has turned out okay. I'm almost done with school, not university, but I'll have a two-year degree. I never would have guessed that. I think after I got my high-school diploma I realized that I could make something out of my life. I had to make something out of my life, for Kaylee's sake.*

I go to school seven hours a week and work thirty hours a week plus homework. Another girl I know lived on welfare while she finished a two-year course to become a beautician. Now she's supporting herself and her child.

Who Will Care for My Baby While I Work or Go to School?

Kaylee stays with my aunt. I want to put her in preschool this year. I just have to find a way to pay for it. Luckily, Head Start has a sliding scale. I think I'll be able to get her in there. I'm hoping if I can schedule school right, I can have her there during my first classes, then bring her home for a break, then go back and finish school for the day. I'll just have to see how it works out. Day care, the kind I really want, is just too expensive.

Melissa found out that day care in her state costs between three hundred and four hundred dollars a month, well above anything she can afford.

I really didn't want to put her in day care at all. My friend's baby is sick all the time. They won't let her bring him when he's sick, but you can't always tell. And the other babies are the same, so in the morning everybody seems healthy, but all it takes is one sneeze to pass on a germ. By that night you've got a room full of sick kids. Then the moms have to stay home from work or school, whatever, and you get way behind, or worse, lose your job. It's really not a good situation, but what can you do?

> **Never leave your baby with someone you do not know or have just met. Get references and check them out.**

Melissa would never leave her child with just anyone: *Oh my gosh, you have to be so careful! Two kids I went to school with had their babies abused by their boyfriends who were baby-sitting. One of the guys went to jail.*

All you have to do is look at the paper. It's in there almost every day: a boyfriend or a baby sitter loses their temper and the baby winds up dead.

My aunt watches Kaylee, and my mom and dad do too. I still trade baby-sitting with my friend, and sometimes my brother will baby-sit, but that's it. They're the only ones I know I can trust.

What Other Help Is Out There?

Melissa found she did not have to depend on welfare to live, but she did receive help from the Special Supplemental Food Program for Women, Infants and Children (WIC) in her state: *WIC gave me formula, and when Kaylee got a little older we got peanut butter, milk, cheese and stuff like that. It really helps.*

She and Kaylee also attended a state-run program called Birth to Three, where mothers with infants and toddlers meet once a week: *I went pretty regularly, especially the first year. It was a*

> **YOU CAN MAKE IT ON YOUR OWN IF . . .**
> ■ you have finished high school.
> ■ you have a job that will support you and your child.
> ■ you have medical insurance.
> ■ you have safe/qualified child care.

relief to have someone to talk to who understood my situation. We had speakers who talked about things like breastfeeding and colic, or what to do if your baby cried all night.

If you really felt stressed out and thought you were going to lose it, you could call someone there, day or night, and they would listen and help if they could.

Can I Live Without Public Assistance?

If, like Melissa, you have a decent-paying job and are willing to sacrifice most of the extras, the answer is yes.

For your own apartment you will need enough money for two months' rent, first and last, plus any cleaning deposit. Don't forget security deposits and installation fees for utilities and phone. There may also be monthly charges for gas, electricity, water, garbage and cable TV.

If you are able to work full time, your employer will most likely provide health insurance. If not, you must consider the cost of doctor visits and medication.

What about transportation? If you have a car, you will need to budget for liability insurance (required by law) and maintenance, including gas, oil and tires.

Reality Check: Research Public Assistance[6]

1. Visit the adult and family service office nearest you, or call the 1-800 number for social services in your state capital. Look in your phone book under

> You will probably need help from your parents or counselor on this one!

"Government Agencies" or "Social Services." Gather information and forms to apply for cash assistance and a Medicaid card. Find answers to the following questions:

> a. How much money do a mother and a child receive?
>
> b. Can you work and receive welfare at the same time?
>
> c. What are the requirements to receive government assistance?
>
> d. How do you qualify for a Medicaid card?

2. At the same appointment, ask about food stamps:

> a. How much do a mother and child receive?
>
> b. What are the requirements?

3. Look in the phone book under "Community Services: Women's Services" for the local WIC office. Call and ask the same questions you asked about food stamps.

4. Use the information you came up with here and in chapter three to complete a monthly budget. Compare that with what you will receive on public assistance.

Expenses		*Public assistance*	
Rent	_____	Welfare	_____
Utilities	_____		
Phone	_____		
Transportation			
Bus	_____		
Car	_____		
Car insurance	_____		
Baby equipment	_____		
Child care	_____		
Food	_____	Food stamps	_____
Health care	_____	Medicaid card	_____
Health			
insurance	_____		
Entertainment	_____		
Total	_____	*Total*	_____

How will you make up the difference?

If you have a job, will you still collect the same amount in welfare benefits?

Job income	_____	Taxes (-20%)	_____
Benefits:			
Insurance	_____	Welfare reduction	_____
Sick pay	_____		

Now what is left to meet the above budget?

7

....

Should I Choose Adoption for My Child?

STOP . . . If you are tempted to skip this chapter, please don't. We are covering all the bases, remember? And yes, adoption is an option. You may not hear about it, but many unwed mothers choose to put their babies up for adoption. Others have it chosen for them later by social services and the courts. How much better it is to explore that option now, before your baby is born.

Jenna was three months pregnant when she chose adoption as her parenting plan: *I wanted to make my decision early on. If I decided to keep the baby I needed to buy diapers, a crib and the works. And if I was going to decide adoption, I needed to start arrang-*

ing my emotions in that direction.

As Jenna discovered, there are more options now than ever before. With regular adoption your baby is placed in a carefully chosen home by an agency or lawyer you trust. This type of adoption is entirely private with no contact whatsoever between you and the adoptive parents. Once an adoption is finalized, the adoptive parents are legally the child's real parents. They assume all the rights and responsibilities for the welfare of the child.

> REASONS TO CHOOSE ADOPTION AS YOUR PARENTING PLAN
> ■ You are very young.
> ■ You are not in a position to care for your child physically, emotionally and financially.
> ■ You are not in a position to marry, and believe your child needs both a father and a mother.

When Jenna contacted the Boys and Girls Aid Society, they explained to her a new method of adoption where the expectant mother chooses her baby's new parents. Her relationship with the baby and his adoptive parents can range from open visits anytime, to a letter and picture once a year, to no contact at all.

Open adoption took away the myth about adoption. I could pick the family that would raise my child. I think that's what made me decide. I wouldn't lose her forever. I would be getting letters and pictures and know that she was safe.

Jenna looked through a book of over fifty carefully screened applicants to determine what kind of family she wanted to raise her baby. All wanted an open adoption, which means they wanted to meet the birth parents and create an ongoing relationship with them. But it was important to Jenna that they also be Christians who would see that her child grew up knowing God.

She chose several families, studied all the information about them, and decided to contact one of them: *Then I got the letter from the Johnsons. They sent a video too. The adoptive mom was everything I wanted to be in ten years. I really believed that God was telling me they were the right ones.*

After Jenna and her mother flew to meet the Johnsons, they were sure these were the right parents for Jenna's child. Even then, however, going through with the adoption was not easy: *It was really a struggle. By that time I was under the impression that all girls should choose adoption. Now, after going through it, I've come to the conclusion it takes a very strong person to deal with that, because in a sense it's like your baby has died. You have that same sense of loss. It really hurts, and not everyone is that strong.*

Jenna is right. Placing your baby in an adoptive home takes courage. It is a sacrifice of love for your child and a gift of love to a childless couple.

Jenna had to ask herself if she could really provide the best parenting for her baby as a single, unemployed teenager or by carefully choosing an adoptive family to raise the child.

Another reason I chose adoption was because I felt

> *Most adoption agencies and services have trained counselors to help you through the adoption process.*

my baby deserved better than food stamps and welfare and secondhand clothes. I didn't want her to feel like she was less of a person, or a mistake. I always wanted her to feel like the blessing and the treasure that she was.

Jenna and her mother both had days when they wondered if they were doing the right thing. Each time they would go down the list of reasons they had made this decision: to provide the baby with a stable home, two parents, financial security, a normal life.

One time we were at the grocery store and there was a lady with a baby. I realized if I was standing there holding my baby, people would say things like "Oh, isn't that a shame? Jenna ruined her life." And "That poor baby." But when the adoptive mother is holding that baby, they'll say, "Oh, isn't that a blessing? Look at that treasure. It's a gift from God."

I don't want my baby to be ashamed. She deserves to feel like a blessing. God created her. And she needs to feel that while she's growing up. And I'm sorry, but it affects a child when they're always looked at with resentment. People see a young girl with a baby and say, "Oh, that's too bad." And that's what the baby lives with her whole life. It's not right.

Making the decision to place your baby in an adoptive home before the baby is born is easier than waiting until the child is older—or having someone else make the decision for you. In Krista's case, Andy was two years old be-

> **YOU CAN GIVE YOUR BABY A STRONG ADOPTIVE HOME IF . . .**
> 1. You do your homework:
>   a. Gather information on adoption.
>   b. Decide which type of adoption, open or closed, is best for you.
> 2. You choose an agency you trust:
>   a. Have someone help you check it out.
>   b. Meet with their staff.
>   c. Share your concerns, hopes and dreams for your child.

fore she realized that they would both have a better future if she placed him in an adoptive home.

When I moved out of my parents' home, I was fifteen and Andy was eighteen months. I couldn't find a job and couldn't keep my grades up in school. I got food stamps and welfare money to pay for rent and diapers, but it was never enough.

Andy was into everything. I couldn't watch him close because I was always so tired. He got outside a couple of times without me knowing. Another lady in my apartment building brought him home. He was fine, but she said I'd better watch it.

I wanted to have some fun. Some time for me, you know? It got so when Andy took a nap, I would lock the door and go out for a while. Anyway, my caseworker came by one night when I wasn't home. Andy was crying, so she went in. I must have forgot to lock the door. They put Andy in a foster home.

The judge put me in a program for alcohol abuse. When I got done, they gave Andy back, but it was worse than before. He screamed all the time. He threw his food and wouldn't take a nap. I couldn't lock him in anymore. He could open anything. Besides, my caseworker might come over again, so I took him with me. My

> **Neglecting your child's needs for food, shelter and safety is a form of child abuse.**

friend and I stopped for beer and I left Andy in the car. When we got back, he was gone.

Andy toddled two blocks before he ran into the street and was struck by a car. Thankfully, his injuries were minor, but they were bad enough to open an investigation. Krista was charged with child abuse. Andy was treated for a broken arm and sent to another foster home.

Krista spent some time at juvenile hall. She was eventually released, but the state would not return Andy until they were certain she could care for him.

Krista felt guilty, but relieved. Without the responsibility of caring for Andy she had more energy and decided to go back to school. A friend brought up the idea of releasing Andy for adoption: *At first I said no way! Andy was my baby. I loved him. Then she warned me I might not have a choice. If I screwed up again, the state would take him away from me for good, and who knows where he would be. It was really hard, but I finally realized there was no way I could give Andy every-*

> **Adoption can make it possible to meet both your needs and those of your child.**

thing he needed. Sure, I loved him. But love can't pay the bills. I wasn't ready to be a parent. I needed to give him a better life.

To be a good parent you don't necessarily have to raise the baby yourself. By letting someone else raise Andy, I am being the best mom I can be.

Krista was too young to give her baby proper care. She needed to learn how to take care of herself first with the right nutrition, adequate sleep and exercise. She needed to finish her education and find a job to support herself before she could think about raising a child.

Carol, Andy's adoptive mother, says: *We love Krista and have agreed that she may visit Andy on his birthdays whenever she can. Still, it's not an ideal situation. She made a hard decision. No one wants to be in that position, but you make the best decision you can. It may not be what your heart wants, but sometimes you have to make a sacrifice.*

The best time to consider adoption is at birth, so the family and baby can have a bonding experience. Physical holding and feeding are important. At two Andy was bonded with his mother whether she took care of him or not. He lost someone and had to grieve. It's a process that affects his personality forever,

> **With parenting there is loss too. The loss of friends and freedom. The loss of future plans and goals.**

whether he remembers his past or not. I wanted to have attachment, but he wouldn't always let me. It took a year of love and patience before he could love us back. This is the risk when you wait.

A friend of Carol's also adopted an older child. She says: *This wasn't the birth mom's decision. She had three babies by three different men. The state had to come in and take the children away. How much better if you choose to release the baby yourself.*

To be able to choose the adoptive parents and have some contact with your baby, at least a letter or a picture—it would give the birth mom peace of mind. You never forget your child. Better to make an educated decision and have the reassurance that your child is well cared for, that you've given a gift to your baby and his or her new family.

If you choose adoption, whether open or closed, you will sign a legally enforceable contract giving the adoptive parents permanent custody of the child. Adoption is a final decision, not temporary foster care, which lasts until you can get back on your feet.

Remember, you are making a decision based on what is best for both you and your baby.

A few years ago, an adoptive mother wrote this letter to her child's birth mother. With her permission I would like to share parts of it with you.

Letter to an Unknown Mother

When you were much younger, you made the most loving decision in your whole life—probably the most difficult. After nurturing an unborn child for nine emotion-packed months, shedding many tears and your own blood, you gave birth to a tiny beautiful son. Then in an act of unspeakable love, you allowed him to become our firstborn.

> IF YOU CHOOSE ADOPTION, YOU WILL NEED QUALIFIED LEGAL HELP FROM ONE OF THE FOLLOWING:
> ■ a public agency (your caseworker will help you)
> ■ a licensed private agency (your counselor or parents will help you)
> ■ an adoption attorney (your counselor or parents will help you)

How we loved and laughed and cuddled him, the precious gift you entrusted to our care. When he smeared his face and hands with his first birthday cake, I thought of you and asked God to comfort and encourage you.

Loving your child has cost us much too, but it was

worth the price. School was always hard for him. College was harder yet, but he was determined to finish. There were no more joyous parents at that commencement than my husband and me. Again tears welled up as I remembered you and your difficult choice.

On the day he placed his strong hand over the trembling hand of his new bride, I asked God to bless you. We had completed our part of the plan. We had helped prepare him to live his life independent of us.

Have you wondered if he thought you didn't love him? We were careful to tell him the immense love it took to make such a hard decision. Because your circumstances prevented you from making a good home, you chose to give that to him the best way you could.

You need never have worried that your son was unwanted. We wanted him long before he was conceived—five childless years.

I read recently there are 1.6 million unfilled requests for adoption annually in the United States, while there are 1.5 million abortions. In the light of these statistics, mothers with your qualities are rare. I grope for words to thank you again for your indescribable gift of love.

With deepest gratitude,
Your son's second mother[7]

Reality Check

1. Get the facts. Contact adoption agencies or services and ask the following questions:

a. What is the cost of adoption? Most or all of

your pregnancy and birth expenses should be covered.

b. Do they have a birth-mother support group?

c. How many adoptive parents are waiting in their pool?

d. Do birth parents choose and meet adoptive parents? Do they exchange identifying informa tion?

e. What services are offered to birth parents and adoptive parents after the placement?

For a list of resources see "Who Can I Call for Help?" on page 103, or look in your local yellow pages under "Adoption."

2. Talk about that information with your counselor or someone from your emotional support group.

3. Think about the atmosphere in which you want your child to be raised, your family relationships, your living situation, your financial outlook, your relationship with the birth father, your access to prenatal care and medical insurance, your goals for the future.

4. Now make a list of pros and cons concerning adoption as a choice. In what ways would adoption be best for you? In what ways would it not? In what ways would adoption be best for your baby? In what ways would it not?

8

....

What If
I Choose
to Raise
My Child?

Carol has worked with teen parents and their babies for several years. She is a birth mother and an adoptive mother. She has this to say to teens who choose to raise their babies: *If you choose to parent, be the best parent you can be. Do the best you can for your child. Stay in school. Stay away from drugs and alcohol. It means giving up being a teenager, but you're not alone. Teen parents are offered more chances and help now than ever before.*

What Does My Baby Need from Me?
If your baby could write you a letter, it might read something like this:

Dear Mommy,

You're the most important person in my world. I'm an awesome responsibility when you consider how helpless I am.

Your tender words and gentle touch nurture my spirit. They're as necessary to my survival as food and breath.

You come when I cry, and keep me fed, warm and dry. I have learned to trust you. When you are kind, honest and truthful, you are teaching me to be the same. Through your discipline and guidance I learn self-control.

With selfless love you allow me to invade every corner of your life. Your reward? My smile and outstretched arms.

Your very presence covers me like a warm blanket; it protects and shields me from harm. When I make you angry, your frown stings. But one forgiving smile heals my broken heart.

With encouragement and pride you watch me grow: first solid food, first steps, first words. You believe in me. When I fall you reach out and help me stand again.

It won't be an easy task to raise me. But when you find you can't handle it on your own, you can ask God for help. I know he loves us both; after all, he gave us to each other.

With the love you taught me,
Your child

How Can I Give My Child the Love He Needs?

Raising children is not easy. Sometimes it is hard to

love them, especially when they want their own way, are openly defiant and do not seem to love us back. It takes maturity. It takes a strength of character we do not have on our own.

In 1 Corinthians 13, the Bible gives us the definition of perfect love. Paul uses words like *patience, kindness, humility, unselfishness* and *self-control.* All qualities it takes to be a good parent. Right? Well, yes. Easy? I don't think so.

Cassie laughs now when she talks about the time she took twelve-month-old Tess into a bookstore: *Tess was whining and twisting in her stroller seat, so I let her get out. She pulled away from me and knocked over a rack of books. It scared her and she started to cry. I picked her up with one hand and tried to stack books with the other. But she still wanted down. She flung herself backwards and just screamed and screamed.*

I was so embarrassed. Everyone in the store was glaring at me. I knew they were thinking, "What are you doing to that baby? Can't you keep that kid under control?" When a clerk came over and offered to clean up the mess, I practically ran out of there. By the time I got back to the car Tess was smiling and jabbering like the whole thing never happened.

By adult standards, Tess's behavior was rude and selfish.

"Wait a minute," you may say; "she was just a baby, she didn't know any better."

You are right. In verse 11 of 1 Corinthians 13, Paul explains, "When I was a child, I talked like a child, I thought like a child, I reasoned like a child. When I became a man, I put childish ways behind me."

Love as defined in the Bible comes with maturity.

Cassie did not swat her daughter, although she was probably tempted. She did not walk away and leave her there, or yell and throw a tantrum of her own. She settled the baby in her car seat and took her home.

Cassie was patient, kind and unselfish. She left without the gift she had gone into the store to purchase. She protected her baby and did not hold a grudge.

Cassie admits: *I stayed awake in child development class, but I'm not a saint; I blow it sometimes.*

We all do. That kind of love does not come naturally. There is only one person who shows perfect love all the time to everyone. His name is Jesus Christ. Not only does he love us like that, but he can help us to love others, including our children, that way too. It is a heart thing, something we allow him to do.

How Can I Help My Child Learn?

How will Tess learn patience, kindness and trust? By watching Cassie and Steve as they let Jesus love her through them. Tess's parents cannot just tell her what is correct behavior; they have to show her.

This poem illustrates what it means to teach by example:

Basic Training

Speak softly
  teach me to listen
Guide gently
  teach me to trust

Show mercy
   teach forgiveness
Judge defiance
   teach respect

Correct kindly
   teach me patience
Laugh often
   teach me joy

Mirror truth
   teach honesty
Model peace
   teach self-control

Brave hardship
   teach me courage
Pursue excellence
   teach me to strive

Gather strength
   grasp hope
Seek God
   teach me to love

Being a parent is a full-time job. You will spend up to eighteen years caring for your child, meeting her needs and training her to live on her own. The goal is to prepare her to become an independent adult. Your baby is born helpless and totally dependent on you, but she will not stay helpless for long. She has much to learn from you.

What Can I Expect When My Child Gets Older?

Melissa was not ready for Kaylee to walk and talk: *I can't believe the difference between an infant and toddler. Oh my gosh. Enjoy them while they're tiny. Infants stay in one place and don't smart off. Toddlers are into everything. They follow you around and ask the same question over and over, and you have to answer them, because how else do they learn?*

Girls who have babies shouldn't expect it to be peachy all the time, because it's not. There are good days, but there are a lot of bad ones. You feel like you can't do it a lot. I go through that all the time.

> TIPS FOR TEEN MOMS
> ■ Sleep when your baby sleeps.
> ■ Keep a schedule.
> ■ Focus on your baby's needs first; when she's content, you will have time for other things.
> ■ Keep up your own health and appearance; you will feel better and so will he.
> ■ Don't try to do it alone; use your resources.
> ■ Don't forget prayer; God is the best resource you've got.

How Can I Plan a Future for Both of Us?

In spite of all the problems, raising Kaylee is working out for me. But I don't think it's the right answer for everyone. I would tell other girls that unless you want to play grownup right now, then I would seriously look into adoption. Because it's a rough life. I've watched a lot of my peers just not make it. You've got to have goals and be willing to do anything to reach them.

Even though Melissa has found that being a parent is tough, she now has goals and can see a future for herself: *If I can just get through school, I want to be a nurse. My labor and delivery nurse was wonder-*

ful. She stayed over to do another shift without pay so she could watch Kaylee be born. She's the reason I chose a nursing career.

Sometimes I feel like I'm fighting a battle by myself. Sometimes I feel like the entire world is against me. Especially now that she's going through this whole two- and three-year-old bit. If it gets any worse I don't know what I'm going to do. When it comes to disciplining and stuff like that, I feel alone. I feel like I'm always the bad guy. And she's not going to love me because I'm always sending her to her room and stuff.

I've heard kids say, "My baby will always love me, no matter what." That's a myth. When I discipline Kaylee she says, "I don't like you. You're mean to me." On the one hand it makes me so mad, and on the other hand it just breaks my heart. Little monster. She plays me like a fiddle sometimes. She knows all the buttons to push.

Should I Raise My Child Alone?
It would be so much better to have someone to share the responsibility of raising Kaylee, but right now I feel like I'm not ready for marriage. I'm still too young. If I do get married I want to be done with school and on my feet financially. That's a big deal to me. And whoever I marry will have to love Kaylee too.

I am finally dating again, but I'm so careful. It's not just me anymore. AIDS, STDs—it's all out there. Some of my friends think, "Well, once I've had sex, I can't stay celibate." But that's not true. They also say, "I won't get pregnant again if I use birth control." Let me tell you, that's not true either. I know lots of girls on welfare, living in slummy apartments, who are pregnant for the second and third time. Not me.

Still, Melissa doesn't try to go it alone. She has learned that being a parent takes work; it does not come naturally: *I call my mom all the time. She's a lifesaver sometimes. I'll be standing there with Kaylee screaming at me and I'm bawling, "Mom, what do I do?"*

Like Melissa, chances are your mother, grandmother or another adult in your life will have parenting skills they would be happy to share. James Dobson, a noted child psychologist, has several books that offer sound, practical advice on child care. Some of them are listed in "What Else Can I Read?" on page 101.

Reality Check: If you have chosen to parent your child . . .

1. Be prepared. Go back to the suggested shopping list in chapter three and make your own. Then start gathering the items you will need when your baby is born. Good sources: your church rummage room, a crisis pregnancy center, a Goodwill or Salvation Army store, secondhand baby stores, friends and relatives willing to pass down baby clothing and supplies. Someone might also throw you a shower.

2. With the help of your counselor or social worker, gather forms and apply for any benefits you may be eligible for.

3. Talk to your doctor now about your baby's health. Learn how to look for signs of physical or neurological problems that might develop as a result

of your or your partner's habits before, during and after pregnancy. Poor nutrition, drinking alcohol, smoking, drug use, sexually transmitted diseases (STDs) and HIV are all factors that affect your child's health.

5. Look at your emotional support list. Find one or two people who will be there when you call day or night to listen or give advice.

6. Post the above numbers by the telephone along with the following: poison control center, your physician, your child's pediatrician and other emergency phone numbers.

7. Buy or borrow books on child care and read them. For suggestions see "What Else Can I Read?" on page 101.

8. Make a list of local organizations that support and help new mothers. For assistance contact your church, counselor or crisis pregnancy center, or look in the phone book under "Social Services" or "Community Services." Call the organizations on your list to see if what they offer will meet your needs. See "Who Can I Call for Help?" on page 103 for additional ideas.

9

How Can I Live with My Choice?

Cassie and Steve got married when Tess was a year old. They do not regret their decision, but choosing to raise Tess meant sacrifices for both of them. Cassie explains: *I gave up my dream of becoming a lawyer. Even after we were married, I was often lonely. Steve was either at school or at work. We never went out. We couldn't afford it.*

Tess is doing great. Steve and I have a good marriage. But I can't take the credit for any of it. Without God, without our parents' love and support, we could never have gotten this far.

Can I Give and Accept Forgiveness?
During the months that Cassie was pregnant, she

realized she had other issues besides their future to resolve: *When I became pregnant I wasn't walking as close to God as I had in the past. Sin separates us from God, especially when we're feeling guilty. Once I was truly able to confess and repent of my sin, I was able to allow God to work through me again and I was able to be at peace.*

> **YOU CAN FEEL GOOD ABOUT DATING AGAIN IF . . .**
> ■ you choose young men with high moral standards.
> ■ you choose young men who show you respect.
> ■ you choose young men with whom you can be honest about your child.
> ■ you both remember that God created sex, but honors it only within the bounds of marriage.
> ■ you both remember that *you are worth waiting for!*

I had always been told that God was a forgiving and loving God. My experience allowed me to realize this in a personal way. It allowed me to rely on his love and power in a new way. I knew if God was a forgiving God then I could forgive myself and expect as well as accept the forgiveness of others.

Jenna talks about forgiveness too, but in a different way: *It's really hard to forgive the father. I'm still struggling with that. Sometimes I have a hard time forgiving myself. I feel really bad because I put everybody through a lot, especially my mother.*

I'm getting ready to get married. I have a child that is not my fiancé's, and that's really hard because sometimes I feel like I'm not good enough for him. But I'm working through it.

Will I Ever Again Feel Good About My Life?

Krista had a hard time working through her problems, but she finally discovered that no matter how tough it gets, there is always a glimpse of hope: *At thirteen and fourteen I made some really poor choices. I thought I had ruined my life forever. Now I see that you do survive.*

I'm dating again—a Christian guy who respects my decision not to have sex. In a few years I'll be ready for marriage. I want to have another baby. Taking care of Andy was hard, but there were a lot of good things too. This time around I'm making better choices.

What If I Choose Adoption?

When Jenna found out she was pregnant, a few friends advised her to have an abortion, while others felt she should parent the baby herself. No one even mentioned adoption: *When I told them I was choosing adoption for my baby, people said things like "You made the mistake,*

> **If you choose the self-sacrificing gift of adoption for your child, be aware that not everyone will agree with your decision.**

you should have to live with the consequences," and "How can you give away your own baby?"

Then a girl in one of my classes said, "You know, Jenna, my mom gave a baby up for adoption, and it was the best thing for her."

This girl really supported my decision. She told me some of the kids were talking about me in English class and the teacher overheard them. She told the class about that story in the Bible, the one where there were two babies and two moms living in the same house. One baby died, and both mothers said, "The live baby is mine!"

They went to King Solomon. He took out his sword and said, "Okay, I'll just split the baby down the middle," because he knew the real mom would give up the baby so it wouldn't be hurt.

That really hit me. This teacher was telling the kids that the mother who really loved the child would do what was best for him. When they heard that, most of the kids started supporting me.

Will I Always Remember My Baby?

After her baby was born, Jenna decided she was going to spend some time with him before she turned him over to the Johnsons: *I needed to see his face and know who he was before I let him go. There were people who were really upset. It wouldn't work for everyone, but I have really good memories of him now.*

Jenna handed the baby over to his adoptive parents and signed the final papers, but on the way home from the hospital she panicked: *I wanted my baby back. I was crying, and my mom said, "Honey, right now our hearts want to go get the baby. We've got to remember that you made your decision and we've had good advice and we've got to hold on to it."*

I knew she was right. I was exhausted, numb. I went in and went to sleep. When I woke up I thought about why I had chosen adoption: "He'll have a daddy and a mommy . . ." I went through the whole list, and I knew I was doing the right thing.

I still had times when I would just burst into tears. They had videotaped the birth. It was a twenty-four-hour labor, very hard. The adoptive parents were there through the whole thing, but they stayed back. They didn't want to interfere. They were wonderful. I didn't see this at the time, but in the videotape my mother hands the baby to Mrs. Johnson. She couldn't have children; this was her first one. When she held the baby, she and her husband, the adoptive father, just stood there, looked at that baby and cried. Just sobbed.

The greatest gift in the whole world is to be a mother, and I was able to give her that gift. I watched that tape, and from that point on I never doubted that we did the right thing.

No one will ever take the place of this baby, but in ten years I can have another one. She could never do that. Some people say I made a mistake. I say, "No, I didn't make a mistake. I did what was right for everyone."

But you don't forget. I have stretch marks from here to here. It's embarrassing. I'm scarred, from a baby I don't have, for the rest of my life. It's a hard thing to grasp. I'll never be able to wear a bikini. I'll never be able to wear a half-shirt.

Some people said to me, "Well, at least this way you get to be young again. At least you still have your life." That's the last thing in the world I wanted to hear, because it isn't true. I just want to shake them and tell them, "You don't understand. That's not why I chose adoption. I wanted this baby. I don't care about my life."

Will My Life Ever Be the Same?

Jenna went back to cheerleading, but it wasn't the same: *When you're pregnant, you grow up. It was really hard because I was in high school. I was a senior, and these girls were driving me crazy.*

Some of the kids were still giving Jenna a hard time because she had chosen adoption. But others understood: *I had lots of friends who were reality checks. Some of them had older babies, two and three years old. They looked at me and said, "I wish I'd had the strength to do it. I see now what everyone was trying to tell me."*

Will I Ever Feel Good About Dating Again?

It took Jenna a year to start feeling normal. She did not have the friends she thought she had. She dropped out of cheerleading. When she tried to date again, it did not work out the way she had hoped: *I started going with this one guy, and he kind of forgot to tell his parents that I'd had a baby. When they found out, that was the end of it.*

Jenna found that because she had had a baby, rejection became a part of life: *I came to a point where I thought, "This is it. It's never going to get any better. My life is over. I might as well just dig a hole and crawl in."*

Then I met Clay. He is wonderful. He loves me, puts up with my moods, buys me anything he can, works as hard as he can; he's incredible, but he wouldn't have dated me if I'd kept the baby. And I don't blame him; he's just being honest. He says that's just too much responsibility for a teenage boy.

Jenna and Clay were married the summer after she graduated, in the same church that supported her through her pregnancy: *The other church kicked* me out. They assumed that because I had said I was getting an abortion, that was how it would be. They never called me later to find out what had happened. Never gave me a chance. For a while I thought all Christians were bad. But the people at this church are wonderful. They're like family, and I thank God for that. The Lord has a special place in this church. You can just feel the warmth when you walk in.

What If I Choose Marriage and It Doesn't Work Out?

Jerry was stationed overseas, and Nichole didn't see him again until Benjamin was almost three: *I raised those babies all by myself. Everybody thought I was terrible for wanting a divorce. "Look at you," my mom said. "How can you do this on your own? Give Jerry time. He'll change."*

I felt really trapped. If I didn't stay married, I'd lose the apartment and part of my allotment. I might have been able to get child support—the navy's pretty good about that—but it wouldn't have been enough. I never did get my high-school diploma. When would I have had time? So welfare was out for me.

When Jerry returned from his tour of duty, he moved back into their apartment: *Benjamin didn't know him, and that made Jerry mad. Like he's suppose to remember a father he hasn't seen since he was one? The baby was terrified of him. We hadn't had any man but their grandpa around in two years.*

I don't know if it will ever work out. The kids need a daddy, but they need to be safe. I need to feel safe. I told Jerry if he ever hits one of us again, I will press charges and leave him. He swears he'll get help. I pray to God that things will change. I love my babies, but sometimes I feel so alone.

Nichole and Jerry eventually got counseling as a family. They still have problems but are now committed to their marriage, their children and God's plan for their lives.

What Will You Choose?

Melissa, Nichole and Cassie chose to raise their babies. Jenna and Krista placed theirs in other loving homes. You have done your homework, acquired a support group and received much counsel. You have the information to make a well-thought-out decision about what is best for your baby.

Remember 1 Corinthians 13? Whether you decide to raise your child yourself or to release her for another family to raise, it will take superhuman love—Christ's love—to succeed. Let Christ love you in a way no one else can. By surrendering your life to Christ, you give him permission to fill you with love for your child, the kind of love that never fails. He has all the strength, power and resources to help you follow through with your decision.

Reality Check

1. Let God love you. He already does, but accepting his love is a choice. Cassie recognized her need for forgiveness. She also knew that God has given us a gift: his son, Jesus Christ. Jesus sacrificed his life so we could come to God. He died and rose again so that we could live forever with God.

2. Get the facts about God's love. Find a Bible and read the Gospel of John. Then read the following verses:

John 3:16, 10:10 (God loves you)

Romans 3:23, 6:23 (we all need a Savior)

Romans 5:8, 1 Corinthians 15:3-6, John 14:6 (the way to God)

John 1:12, Ephesians 2:8-9, John 3:1-8 (accepting God's gift)

Romans 8:28, 31-39 (secure in God's love)

3. Ask questions. Talk about these verses with your Christian counselor, your pastor or another Christian on your support list. Both Cassie and Jenna talked to their pastor's wife.

This is probably the most difficult time of your life. The good news is, you don't have to go it alone. The choice is yours.

....

Just for
Parents

"Mama, I think I'm pregnant."
Words that crush your spirit, rock your world. You
are feeling hurt, angry, humiliated, betrayed. Your
feelings are valid, and you are not alone.

I hope you have been reading this book along with
your daughter. If so, you will recognize Jenna's
situation. Here is some of what her mother has to
say: *We lay there and cried the night she told me. I
was so sure she was wrong. She'd start her period
any day and everything would be all right.*

*Jenna's pregnancy represented the death of her
childhood. I felt numb. I tried to talk to other people,
but nobody can understand how you feel unless*

they've gone through it themselves.

I called a friend who had two daughters who had gotten pregnant. When I told her that Jenna was pregnant, there was a long silence. Then she said, "It hurts, doesn't it?" and we cried together. I needed someone to tell me that what I was feeling was normal.

I kept saying, "If I had only done this or that, she wouldn't be pregnant now. She doesn't have a father, and I'm never home." My friend said, "Both of my girls had a loving, caring father, and I never worked. What was our excuse?" I needed to hear that too.

Jenna kept telling me, "Mama, it's not your fault." But somehow I felt I'd failed her.

That Sunday when I went forward for prayer, the lady in charge of the crisis pregnancy center came up, put her arm around me and said, "I know what you're going through. I went through it too, and I was a pastor's wife." We cried together. God knew I needed someone to put their arms around me and to hold me.

Jenna's mother did not agree with her daughter's decision to have an abortion. Still, she made it known she would support her with love and prayer: *I really believed this was between Jenna and God. And it was real hard when she was considering abortion. A few days before the appointment, I said "Honey, I'll still love you, but I'm so sorry, you'll have to find your own way."*

> **Denial is one of the first stages of grief.**

My sister agreed to take her, but she had had an abortion several years before, and Jenna's situation broke open a lot of wounds. In the end my sister had to say, "I just can't take you." I think that was a catalyst toward Jenna making the decision not to follow through.

While Jenna struggled with her choices—to try and raise the baby or place it with an adoptive family—her mother went through the same agony of indecision: *I didn't know what to do, because I wanted my daughter to be happy, you know, but I knew in my heart of hearts what needed to be done. I think the key is that I had people who supported me and prayed for me and loved me. That way I could support my daughter.*

Another mother found that being honest about her own feelings was the key to preserving her relationship with her daughter: *When my daughter told me she was pregnant, my first reaction was fear. As a single parent who raised four children alone, I was so afraid I'd have to raise another one. There was so much pain in raising this child that I just couldn't help telling God, "I can't do it, Lord." In time, my daughter and I talked of my fears. She knew I could not fill in if she slipped up.*

> **Acquire your own support group. Don't try to cope alone.**

I had no part in her decision. When we talked and she struggled with the choices, I told her, "Whatever decision you make, there will be serious hard times. If I try and sway you one way or another, when the hard times come, you will have the option to blame me. You need total ownership of this decision. But whatever one you make, I will support you the best I know how."

By assuring her daughter of her love and support, this mother allowed her daughter to accept responsibility for her own choices.

An unexpected pregnancy can be just as hard on the father's parents. One mother talks about their reaction to the news: *I guess we were lucky in that our son and his girlfriend had known each other for years. We knew her and her family well.*

The kids thought they had been through the hard part when they told her parents. Her mom was upset, of course, but she was able to focus on the coming baby. Our son told me later he wasn't prepared for our reaction.

His dad and I were devastated and so angry with him. We were amazed that he could have been so stupid. As parents you spend all those years doing everything you can to give them a good life and prepare them for the future. When they turn around and take all that effort and trash it, you feel so helpless.

We had done everything we could to protect him from just this situation. We had talked with him, been open and honest from the time he was little and first started asking questions. He was well educated. One night of rampaging hormones, and all our dreams, all our hopes for our son's future, were gone.

You think and think, "What did I do wrong? What could I have done differently?" You raise them to make their own choices, and hope they're strong enough to face the consequences. But when that time comes, you suffer from their mistakes.

Still, the young man's parents supported his and his girlfriend's decision to marry: *I was fortunate that I was allowed to be in the room when our grandchild was born. Such a miracle! And I didn't have to do any of the work. I could really enjoy this birth.*

It was wonderful to watch our son become a father. He did not take it lightly. He was in awe, amazed and ecstatic about this child of his. I'll never forget when he handed his baby to his dad. That was a special moment in my life.

Now we see how our boy has matured. We didn't think he would deal with things as well as he has. He's working hard, but most of all we see him being a good daddy. The baby's face lights up when she sees him. There's a lot of hope there. A lot of love and caring. Maybe that future we thought was destroyed will be okay after all.

For Jerry's mom, the outcome has not been as good: *When the kids got married, the wedding was very hard. Everybody smiling, congratulating us. It's hard to smile and be polite when you want to just crawl off into a corner and cry.*

Jerry wasn't used to so much responsibility. He had to buckle down and make some money. It's hard to see your son still trying to figure out why all of a sudden he not only has to take the garbage out, but he has to protect this wife who's going through pregnancy mood swings. They're trying to build a marriage and deal with all the physical problems of a pregnancy at the same time. It's hard to watch them struggle—and they do.

In spite of Nichole and Jerry's problems, Nichole's mother says she would not trade those babies for anything: *You have this grandbaby—in my case, two—who if given a chance is going to love you. And believe me, you are going to love that baby. They may not get here quite the way you want, but when they are here they are a real blessing.*

For another girl's mother, the hardest part was telling her own parents: *It's hard to tell the soon-to-be great-grandparents. They have their hopes and dreams wrapped up in this child too. It's almost like calling your mommy and daddy and telling them that you failed. It's so hard to hear the hurt in their voices. My mother sobbed.*

It seems as parents we're always paying consequences for our kids' behavior. Just as we did for our own.

Mom and Dad, you are not alone. God is your strength and shield. Your help in every kind of trouble. Just as he can help your child make the best decisions possible, he can comfort you and give you all the wisdom and strength you will need in the coming months.

Ideas for Counselors: How to Use This Book

Whatever your relationship to a pregnant teen—her pastor, counselor, parent, concerned relative, caring friend—you have one goal: to help her. This book was written with that in mind.

In chapter one, each pregnant teen is asked to compile a list of people she can turn to for emotional support. You are likely one of them. If you are a professional, you may already know that a girl in this situation, if she is past the denial stage, is worried about the crisis at hand and what she is going to do about it right now, this minute. She is scared, perhaps angry, probably feeling sick and under a great deal of emotional stress. She needs an adult she can trust: a calm, interested, nonjudgmental person to listen, offer advice and guide her in making the best decisions possible for her and her child.

Cassie and Jenna went to their pastor's wife for counsel. Both girls were able to make intelligent, well-thought-out decisions because someone in the very beginning was willing to listen and give advice when asked for it.

There were times, Jenna says, when she wanted to give up and an adult friend offered encouragement. For example, some days she felt too sick to ride the bus, and a teacher took the time to pick her up and take her to school.

Krista says she might have made different choices, ones that would have spared her and her baby a lot of pain, if someone had been with her to help her understand the options.

More than one crisis pregnancy counselor or pastor has walked a trembling teen to her parents' door and stood by with emotional support while the girl owned up to her condition. If this is your role, you may be working with the girl's family as well.

What Now? Help for Pregnant Teens has been designed as a tool for you to help the girl, and perhaps her partner and parents as well, evaluate the present and explore the future. Its aim is not to dictate but to direct. Each chapter has a "Reality Check" section with questions to answer and information for the teen to think about.

Suggestions for Pastors and Counselors

In a one-on-one situation, you might encourage the

teen to read the chapters, then talk about the questions and responses together. She may need help finding resources, locating phone numbers and addresses of support agencies, or finding a doctor. She may need a lot of encouragement in following through with the decision-making process.

In a group situation, the chapters could be assigned as homework and responses to the questions evaluated at the next meeting. Hearing other girls' responses might clue a teen to an option she may not have previously considered. The material can be covered in eight or nine sessions.

In this book, teen mothers share their stories because they want to help someone else benefit from their mistakes. They want to offer encouragement ("your life isn't over") and a caution ("the decisions you make now will affect both you and your baby for the rest of your lives").

This book is intended as a decision-making guide for pregnant teens. A teen could read and assimilate the material on her own, but as Proverbs says, "Plans fail for lack of counsel, but with many advisors they succeed" (15:22).

God bless you as you endeavor to guide a troubled teen through these pages. And thank you for caring.

What Else Can I Read?

Adoption

Caplin, Lincoln. *An Open Adoption.* New York: Farrar, Straus & Giroux, 1990.

Lindsay, Jeanne Warren. *Open Adoption: A Caring Option.* Buena Park, Calif.: Morning Glory, 1987.

Sifferman, Kelly Allen. *Everything You Need to Know Before You Call a Lawyer: The Layman's Guide to Adoption.* 2nd ed. Hawthorne, N.J.: Career Press, 1994.

Silber, Kathleen, and Phylis Speedlin. *Dear Birth Mother.* 2nd ed. San Antonio, Tex.: Corona, 1991.

Pregnancy

Eisenberg, Arlene, Heidi E. Murkoff and Sandee E.

Hathaway. *What to Eat When You're Expecting.* New York: Workman, 1986.

──────. *What to Expect When You're Expecting.* 2nd ed. New York: Workman, 1991.

Baby and Child Care

Carter, John Mack, ed. *The Good Housekeeping Illustrated Book of Pregnancy and Baby Care.* New York:: Dorling Kindersley/Hearst Books, 1990.

Dobson, James. *Dare to Discipline.* 2nd ed. Wheaton, Ill.: Tyndale House, 1992.

──────. *Parenting Isn't for Cowards.* Dallas: Word, 1987.

Eisenberg, Arlene, Heidi E. Murkoff and Sandee E. Hathaway. *What to Expect the First Year.* New York: Workman, 1989.

Sears, William and Martha. *The Baby Book.* Boston: Little, Brown, 1993.

Fathers

Reynolds, Marilyn. *Too Soon for Jeff.* Buena Park, Calif.: Morning Glory, 1994.

....

Who Can
I Call for
Help?

Even if you have already estab-lished a support group, you may want extra help. These phone numbers will help you locate the crisis pregnancy center or Christian counseling center nearest you.

    1. Care Net National Help Line: 1-800-395-HELP (crisis pregnancy hotline)

    2. Bethany Christian Services: 1-800-BETHANY (crisis pregnancy hotline)

    3. Holt International Children's Services: 1-800-234-HOLT (adoption and pregnancy counseling)

    4. Boys and Girls Aid Society: 1-800-342-6688 (adoption counseling)

5. Open Adoption and Family Services: 1-800-772-1115 (open adoption counseling)

For financial aid or support services, such as WIC, Birthright or Birth to Three, look in the community services section of your phone book.

Notes

[1]Statistic from Oregon governor's office as published in the *Register Guard,* March 22, 1996.

[2]Lynn Johnston, *For Better or for Worse,* February 12, 1997.

[3]Author unknown.

[4]Some of these questions and instructions are adapted with permission from Sheri Levine, *Connecting with Teens* (Portland, Ore: Open Adoption & Family Services, 1996).

[5]Statistic from Oregon governor's office as published in the *Register Guard,* March 22, 1996.

[6]Some of these questions are adapted with permission from Sheri Levine, *Connecting with Teens* (Portland, Ore: Open Adoption & Family Services, 1996).

[7]Marjorie Gordon, "Letter to an Unknown Mother," 1988. Excerpts used by permission.